ESSENTIAL **DK** MANAGERS

MANAGING
CHANGE

ROBERT HELLER

Lond   cow

A DORLING KINDERSLEY BOOK

Project Editor Catherine Rubinstein
Project Art Editor Elaine C. Monaghan
Editor Felicity Crowe
Designers Simon J. M. Oon, Adam Powers

DTP Designer Jason Little
Production Controllers Silvia La Greca,
Michelle Thomas

Series Editor Jane Simmonds
Series Art Editor Tracy Hambleton-Miles

Managing Editor Stephanie Jackson
Managing Art Editor Nigel Duffield

First published in Great Britain in 1998
by Dorling Kindersley Limited,
9 Henrietta Street,
London WC2E 8PS

A CIP catalogue record for this book is available
from the British Library

ISBN 0 751 306339

Reproduced by Colourscan, Singapore
Printed and bound in Italy by Graphicom srl

CONTENTS

IMPLEMENTING CHANGE

CONSOLIDATING CHANGE

INTRODUCTION

Change is the single most important element of successful business management today. To remain competitive in increasingly aggressive markets, organizations (and individuals in them) have to adopt a positive attitude to change. Ignoring or trivializing a changing trend can be costly, so Managing Change teaches managers how to be one step ahead of rivals, set trends, and lead change in order to survive. Techniques for planning and implementing change, for example, are explained clearly, to help you maximize potential gain. Practical advice is given on how to achieve the best from staff by using their strengths and involving them at all stages, while 101 concise tips scattered throughout the book give further vital information. Finally, a self-assessment exercise allows you to evaluate and improve your change-management skills.

UNDERSTANDING CHANGE

Understanding and managing change are the dominant themes of management today. Adapting to the ever-changing present is essential for success in the unpredictable future.

WHY CHANGE?

Change affects every aspect of life: taking a proactive approach to change is the only way to take charge of the future, either as an individual or as an organization. Approach it with an open mind, and learn to develop its positive elements.

1 Write down any changes you would like – and plan for them.

2 If you find you are resisting change, ask yourself why.

BEING OPEN TO CHANGE

For organizations, change is the way to stay competitive and to grow. For individuals, the opportunities created by change enrich careers and personal lives. You can deal with change in three ways: by resisting, following, or leading. A resister tries to stay put, which is impossible in changing situations; the majority of people and organizations who start by resisting eventually find they have to follow, trying to catch up – if that fails, they face competitive disadvantage. Seeking to anticipate and lead change is thus, paradoxically, safer as well as more adventurous.

SEEING THE EFFECTS

Positive aspects of change may be less obvious at first than negative ones. New ventures, expansion, promotions, and booms often bring challenges before delivering gains. Cases such as departmental or factory closures, dismissals, bankruptcies, or deterioration in markets bring difficulties and very few immediate benefits. But, however it appears, approach change positively as potential opportunity. Use it as a stimulus to encourage new ideas and harness enthusiasm for further progress.

3 Seek out people who welcome change, and become their ally.

CHANGING NATURALLY

People live with change constantly: in a lifetime, everyone goes through personal transformation from infancy to adolescence, young adulthood, middle age, and finally old age. A career path may lead from subordinate to junior management, middle management, and eventually board level or consultancy. Organizations also mature and evolve, with major changes on many levels in policy and practice. For personal satisfaction and career progress, increase your capacity to change.

4 Think before following the same policy as everyone else.

▲ OLD ASSEMBLY LINE

Mass production revolutionized manufacturing. While still labour intensive, manual work became relatively quick, clean, and less physically demanding, enabling women to work in previously male-dominated areas.

▲ MODERN ASSEMBLY LINE

Modern production lines bear only the slightest resemblance to older versions. Technological breakthroughs and economies of scale have radically reduced the ratio of staff to machines.

UNDERSTANDING THE CAUSES OF CHANGE

To deal effectively with increasing rates of change, you need to understand the underlying causes. Specific changes in an organization's internal structure and external markets often derive from wider changes in society, economics, or technology.

> **5** Respond positively to uncertainty rather than avoid change.

> **6** Cultivate curiosity: try to become the best-informed person you know.

SOCIAL CAUSES

General trends in society, politics, and demography touch everyone. In recent years these have resulted in upsurges in the youth and consumer markets, a shift in emphasis from community to a more individual-centred society, and ageing populations. Businesses are affected by such trends, which influence consumer demand and other economic patterns. Managers need an informed awareness of changes and their reasons. Reading material on social and political issues, and drawing conclusions from what you read and observe, will help you deal with changing trends and even predict them.

CHANGING MODELS ▼
Office equipment has developed rapidly since the invention of the typewriter. Today's personal computers can perform tasks that were unimaginable 100 years ago.

Keys operated typebars manually

MANUAL TYPEWRITER

"Golfball" typing head and electric motor were revolutionary

ELECTRIC TYPEWRITER

ECONOMIC CAUSES

The tides of economics change quite slowly, but with inexorable power. Within their relatively stable trends, however, markets and monetary flows can fluctuate sharply, competitive ways can alter dramatically, and technology and innovation can fracture established patterns. This compels organizations to be ready to adjust to sudden change on any level. But it is also prudent for managers to have basic contingency plans and funds to call on during periods of uncertainty.

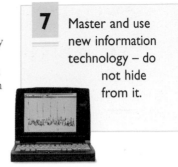

7 Master and use new information technology – do not hide from it.

TECHNOLOGICAL CAUSES

At accelerating speed, the revolution in information technology (IT) is having a profound impact on methods of management, manufacture, service, purchasing, and selling. IT is part of a drive to accomplish current tasks more efficiently (for instance, to control stocks more accurately) and to achieve new purposes (such as space travel). Managers need the former for competitive survival and the latter for competitive success. Try to maintain an informed openness to technological developments, since new technologies that appear irrelevant at first may be the next winner.

8 Bear in mind that technology is changing more and more quickly.

Increased range of functions became available

Screen and processor were added to keyboard

EARLY COMPUTER

Streamlined machine has many functions and large memory

MODERN COMPUTER

RECOGNIZING SOURCES OF CHANGE

Change can come from many directions: from superiors or subordinates within an organization, from personal initiative, and from outside. Make sure that you are aware of all the possible sources, and be open to change, wherever it comes from.

9 Welcome change initiatives from all sources.

CHANGING FROM WITHIN

Most changes that occur in an organization are instigated, at least in part, from within. The majority of these changes are minor: for example, requiring a new report or modifying a tender. However, most sizeable changes, such as restructuring and acquisitions, are generated from the topmost level, and generally unexpected by subordinate staff. As a manager, you initiate changes yourself, but are also often required to act as a link between different levels of staff. Ensure that the system does not prevent the ideas of subordinates from being heard.

SENIOR MANAGER

Manager proposes initiatives to higher levels

Superior passes initiatives down, allowing scope for further input

Decisions affect or are affected by other divisions or external contacts

MANAGER

Manager implements initiatives, and encourages further discussion

Subordinates propose initiatives upwards

FACILITATING CHANGE ▶
The manager is the focal point of change. He receives suggestions and reacts to initiatives from above and below, and works proactively in both directions.

SUBORDINATES

RESPONDING TO RIVALS

The skill of managers is revealed by their response to external change. If a rival manufacturer launches a new product or cuts costs, a passive manager, rather than alter established working practices, ignores the change or denies its significance. A strong manager, on the other hand, seizes the chance to re-examine the market or production processes to better the rival's actions. Better still, a proactive manager anticipates competitors and acts to instigate the winning change themselves.

10 Always respond positively to changes outside your organization.

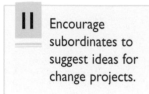

11 Encourage subordinates to suggest ideas for change projects.

RESPONDING TO CONTEXTS

An organization's markets affect its changes. In fast-moving trades, managers are accustomed to instigating change, and are more likely to restructure internally at frequent intervals and be open to experimental practices. The ownership of the organization also influences attitudes to change: in a public firm you may come under pressure from investors to change. On the other hand, a private company may allow you to make a risky but brilliant experimental change.

LOOKING AT PERSONALITY

Your character affects your propensity to change. A passive, shy, and cautious person is unlikely to become an enthusiastic promoter of change. This is a natural role for a proactive, self-confident risk-taker. But change demands followers as well as leaders. Try to discover which personality type best describes each member of staff, and use this information to obtain optimum results from your team. Once momentum has been established, each individual can make a contribution in their own way. This becomes evident in crises, when everybody works to the best of their ability to achieve radical change in the interests of survival.

QUESTIONS TO ASK YOURSELF

Q Over the last 12 months, what significant changes have I personally made?

Q Do I try to anticipate external changes and act on my findings?

Q Have I contributed to any internal change programmes?

Q Do I listen to ideas for change coming from below?

Q Do I react positively to demands for change?

CATEGORIZING TYPES OF CHANGE

*C*hange divides broadly into gradual and radical forms. Within these, a wide variety of types and combinations occur. Understanding the type you are dealing with will help you to approach change effectively and to interpret others' response to it.

12 Consider the combined effects of different types of change.

ANALYZING CHANGE

Both gradual and radical change may be either reactive or proactive, according to whether you make the change voluntarily or in response to the pressure of other developments. In practice, change often combines reactive and proactive elements. For instance, a crisis triggers radical reactive change in response to a calamity, but you have to decide proactively on the direction of the change in order to maximize the organization's long-term success.

13 When analyzing change, look at both short- and long-term contexts.

GRADUAL CHANGE

A gradual change is a change that occurs slowly over a prolonged period, at a steady rate or with minor fluctuations in intensity. It can involve many people or just a few, but is most effective as an unending organization-wide change programme to improve quality of products and processes, reduce costs, and raise productivity. Even small improvements can make powerful savings. Radical change may occur at the same time, either hand-in-hand with gradual change or independently.

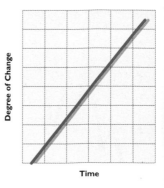

GRADUAL CHANGE ▶
Company-wide changes are implemented at a steady rate over a prolonged period of time.

Degree of Change

Time

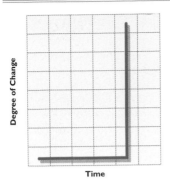

▲ RADICAL CHANGE

After a relatively stable, even stagnant period, one or more major changes are introduced at a single stroke.

RADICAL CHANGE

A radical change is a sudden, dramatic change with marked effects – for example, reversing company strategy to tap a new market. The change may be commercial or structural, although the two tend to go together: it is often, but not always, large-scale. Just as a big, risky stock-market investment has both more to gain and more to lose than a small, cautious one, so successful organizations stand to gain most from radical change. Yet the fact that an organization has been successful up to now may make it hard for people to accept a radical change. Before making radical changes of any kind, plan thoroughly, thinking through the options in detail to minimize risks.

CRISIS MANAGEMENT

Managing a crisis inevitably means making radical changes to avert catastrophe. A change is best led by one person or a small group who can take decisions and act rapidly after a quick analysis of critical needs. Nothing is sacrosanct. Closing a treasured head office, for instance, will save money and symbolize change. Full communication with everybody is often a big change. So is the urgency with which a crisis programme is pushed through.

 14 Learn from crises, to prevent them from recurring.

CULTURAL DIFFERENCES

Japan industrialized extremely quickly: continual, proactive change is part of Japanese culture. Continental Europeans are traditionally reactive, but are starting to instigate change. The British, once conservative, were converted to proactive change by national crises. Americans became more proactive towards change in the 1990s, thanks partly to the micro-electronics industry.

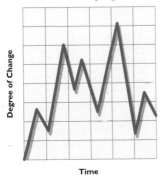

◀ CRISES

In the absence of a comprehensive plan, change shows a rollercoaster pattern. Dramatic action in response to each crisis is followed by a marked fall-off, until the next crisis is triggered.

13

CHANGING WITH GROWTH

Growth is change: as an organization expands, change is inevitable. The adjustment may be a gradual process, a series of radical jumps, or most often a combination of the two. Some changes are natural and relatively easy. As people learn new skills, for example, their performance naturally improves with repetition. Other changes may be much more difficult. For instance, as a small business expands, it typically grows beyond the owner's existing management ability. Some owners can accomplish the transformation from proprietor to professional manager successfully, but many do not. All businesses have their limits to growth, which cannot be transcended without considerable change. Plan any growth carefully, keeping it to levels you can cope with. If you do not, the organization – be it large or small – will sooner or later crack under the strain.

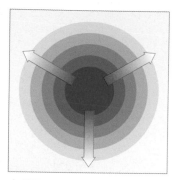

▲ CHANGE THROUGH EXPANSION

As an organization grows, jobs tend to expand in scope as well as number. This means that many people have to adjust to more complex management structures.

CHANGING TO WIN

Many changes in business, both gradual and radical, are driven by a desire to gain advantage and beat the competition. Some advantages – more resources, more customers, and often lower costs – come with growth. But other factors may also help provide a winning edge: technology, service, distribution, productivity, marketing, and financing. They may yield lower costs and prices, too. Any function can hold the key, if you dare to be different. If everyone in your industry is stuck in the same pattern, search for changes that will be welcomed by customers and will enable you to stand out. Prepare for times when only radical change can meet major market or other trends; anticipate and overcome limits to growth; be willing to change anything and everything to enhance your competitive prowess.

QUESTIONS TO ASK YOURSELF

Q What changes would I hope to see in a year's time?

Q What changes have been introduced in the last year, and how successful have they been?

Q Am I keeping up with developments in the market, the industry, and technology?

Q Do I encourage staff to generate ideas for change?

Q What radical changes would make the most difference to this organization?

Q Am I learning continuously – and ensuring that other people do the same?

15 Aim to equal or surpass the best examples you find.

 **16** Be different and better than the competition if you want to be the winner.

CHANGING INTRINSICALLY

Learning to change may, in many cases, constitute a major change in itself. One of the best ways to establish a new, adaptable way of thinking and working is to develop a "learning organization". This is an organization in which change-oriented thinking becomes a habit for everybody, and so change – gradual and at times radical as well – is always under way, with all processes and systems intrinsically subject to constant review. This kind of approach facilitates the development of the organization and ensures that it is well prepared for crisis management in cases of emergency. For major changes (especially fundamental changes in ways of thinking) to be effective, however, they must extend to everyone and everything. All too often, enormous change is made in parts of an organization, but because other areas are not involved, and have not changed, success is limited.

COMBINING CHANGES

In practice, most change involves a combination of change types, or progression from one sort to another. A process may be largely reactive, as when initial radical response to a crisis gives way to a gradual follow-up programme. Or the whole project may be proactive and systematic, as in Total Quality Management (TQM) programmes. These introduce various types of needed change simultaneously, covering systems, processes, people, and management. To ensure that change is lasting and effective, there must be practical improvement of operations and at the same time a change in ways of thinking among both managers and staff. This is a challenge for any organization. The task is even more complex because priorities alter with circumstances: reassessing the need for change is a key to changing successfully.

POINTS TO REMEMBER

- Limits to growth must be recognized: growth should not be forced beyond them.
- Changes that give clear competitive advantage are particularly desirable.
- Changes made in isolation will often have disappointing results.
- Valuable changes in thinking by managers and staff will be revealed by changes in behaviour.
- In reviewing internal processes and performance, a sense of discontent may be put to constructive use.
- All changes should bring direct or indirect benefits to customers and employees.

PLANNING CHANGE

Successful change programmes always involve
planning – for both the short and the long term.
The clearer the objectives, the better the plan.

FOCUSING ON GOALS

*If managers do not know where they are
going, they cannot change to get there.
If they do not know where they are, they
cannot start on the right road. Establish
these start and finish points as a first step
in identifying where changes are needed.*

17 Realistically assess
your organization's
strengths and
weaknesses.

18 Keep your vision
statements to one
or two short
sentences.

ASSESSING OBJECTIVES

Most businesses, like most people, have unclear
ambitions or none at all. Forming and clarifying
objectives, either as an organization or as an
individual, can have powerful results – many
companies have turned their fortunes around
merely by focusing their corporate aims. Your
goals should be high but realistic, with the
emphasis on "high": even the most apparently
far-fetched dreams can sometimes be realized.
Express your dreams in words, then convert those
words into facts and figures, and you will have a
sound basis for planning how to achieve them.

EXPRESSING PRINCIPLES

Ambitions expressed in words are known as "visions" – for example, the desire to be the market leader in personal financial services. Visions break down into "missions", such as aiming for a certain ranking in life insurance. Make sure that visions and missions are consistent with long-term "values", the principles on which an organization bases its decisions and actions. Keep these long-term values practical, and make visions, missions, and values as simple and concise as possible, avoiding high-flown language. Being clear about these aims will help to identify changes needed.

IDENTIFYING GAPS

A strategic gap often looms not only between where you are now and where you want to be, but also between your present capabilities and those that your ambitions require. Measure present states ruthlessly: assessing the present is one area in which near-total objectivity and certainty are possible. Then use your judgment to relate the present to your desired ends, working back from future to present. Plotting change in this way, as a means to a predetermined end, is often highly effective, and will help you to measure progress.

SETTING YOUR SIGHTS

Ask "Where are we now?" Assess from various viewpoints

Ask "Where do we want to be?" Develop a corporate vision

Measure the gap between the present and the ideal state. Quantify it tangibly

Map out key changes needed to close the gap, working back from the ideal

State these changes in words and figures as a focus for planning change

19 Change corporate culture through individuals, not vice versa.

ASSESSING CULTURE

Understanding corporate culture is crucial when planning for change. An organization's long-term aims can be achieved only if staff are in sympathy with them and with each other. Study the corporate culture to see how best to introduce changes, as well as how to encourage personal values to align with organizational ones and develop people's openness to change. Changing corporate culture is notoriously difficult, but positive, lasting change in culture should follow from other changes.

IDENTIFYING THE DEMAND FOR CHANGE

Success hinges on pleasing customers: dissatisfied customers will find other suppliers. Unhappy employees – effectively internal "customers" – work poorly or leave. Use surveys to monitor requirements in both groups, then plan changes to satisfy them.

20 Strive to satisfy the needs of both employees and customers.

21 Cherish customers who complain: they tell you what to change.

USING DISSATISFACTION

Make the most of feedback when planning change. Customers are always right: if they believe your product to be inferior, that belief is valid, even if tests prove it false. The same is true of employees, your internal customers. In both cases, use surveys (via questionnaires, focus groups, or interviews) to explore perceptions – dissatisfied people do not always voice their complaints unasked.

ASKING CUSTOMERS

Each product or service has many aspects. Use surveys to find out which matter most to the customers – the results will almost certainly contradict assumptions you might have made.

When carrying out a survey, extend your market research to your competitors, and compare customer opinion on them with the customer response to your own organization. This will show where changes are required for greatest impact on customers. Follow up with further surveys after implementing change plans.

MEASURING CUSTOMER ▼ DISSATISFACTION

This pie chart is based on surveys showing the different problems that contributed to customers' dissatisfaction with a telephone service. Bad sales service and faulty equipment accounted for most customer dissatisfaction, so these areas became the main focus of change.

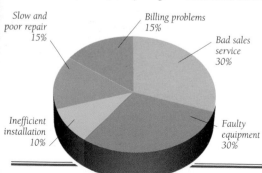

Slow and poor repair 15%

Billing problems 15%

Bad sales service 30%

Inefficient installation 10%

Faulty equipment 30%

ASSESSING QUALITY

Customer requirements for quality are a good basis for starting to plan change. Total Quality Management (TQM) looks at how every element of a business process contributes to the whole. Apply this approach to help identify ways to satisfy customers. At the same time, use quality control methods to run internal checks (such as number of defects per million parts). Remember, there is no point in improving quality on unwanted products, or in making desired products inefficiently.

22 Remember that quality of product depends on quality of process.

ASKING EMPLOYEES

Organizations depend for success on their employees. You need a high level of employee satisfaction if the firm is to perform at its best – dissatisfied employees will soon leave or, worse, perform badly. Conduct surveys, both qualitative and quantitative, among employees as you do among customers, and involve employees in identifying any need for change. This will raise morale and help you improve quality of processes.

23 Use objective measures of customer response.

CONDUCTING A SURVEY

To get the most from a survey – by post, in person, or by phone – plan thoroughly or use a professional consultant.

● Keep questionnaires short and simple.
● Avoid questions that influence answers.
● Avoid vague measures ("very satisfied") and long scales ("1 to 10").
● Be definite ("Would you use this?"), with few options ("yes", "maybe", "no").
● Make sure you ask appropriate people.
● Be sure that the sample and response rate produce a statistically valid result.

▲ **SURVEYING EFFECTIVELY**
Prepare questions thoroughly before beginning a survey, and have all necessary equipment to hand. Inefficiency is off-putting for interviewees.

SELECTING ESSENTIAL CHANGES

Change programmes must be fully comprehensive if they are to last. But be careful not to overwhelm people with too many specific changes: identify the few significant priority areas in which change will have most impact, and focus on these.

24 Prioritize change in key areas, then focus attention more widely.

CHOOSING KEY AREAS

Pareto's Law holds that roughly 20 per cent of activities account for 80 per cent of problems: aim to identify and concentrate on these key areas to maximize the impact of change. You can determine your starting point by addressing urgent needs, but do not forget other areas when assessing the most significant aspects, and do not allow the principle "if it ain't broke, don't fix it" to inhibit initiatives: processes that appear to be working well may in fact need improvement. Bear in mind, too, that an organization's activities are all interdependent, and should not be approached in isolation.

JUSTIFYING CHANGES

Support your proposed changes by making a business case for them. You are not changing for change's sake, but for a purpose. Analyze every aspect to show why and where change is required to reach objectives, the areas in which change is likely to have greatest impact, and what that impact is likely to be. Having fully justified the priorities of your proposals, you can then decide to make changes in other areas, too, provided sufficient resources and time are available.

25 Be clear about the purpose of any change you plan to make.

AVOIDING OVERLOAD

One important reason for selecting essential changes is that if you introduce too many new initiatives in close succession, staff may suffer from overload. "Initiative fatigue" reveals itself rapidly in falling performance, high stress levels, low morale, and diminishing return on initiatives. Reversing an initiative, once launched, is extremely difficult, so keep careful control over the number and intensity of planned changes, and consult staff fully.

26 Concentrate on a few processes that really count.

▼ **TOO MUCH CHANGE**
A few changes can make all the difference between a boring work environment and a stimulating one. Too many, however, may leave the workforce overwhelmed.

| BORED | STIMULATED | OVERWHELMED |

Increasing Amount of Change

27 Plan a fluid, integrated change programme.

MAINTAINING CONTINUITY

Ideally, aim to create an overall programme for change, continually renewed, within which many projects move forward simultaneously. It is bad change management to halt one initiative and begin another before the first has had a chance to work: this type of "flavour of the month" approach breeds cynicism and apathy. Prepare for change well, with full consultation, so that people know what will happen and can plan their workload.

◀ **CREATING CHAOS**
An old rule states that more than one objective is no objective. To avoid chaos, a change programme must focus on a single overriding target, selecting and structuring other changes around it.

CASE STUDY
Henry took over a lagging business and decided on total change. He dropped many products and services, introduced new ones, moved from selling through wholesalers to selling direct to retailers, reorganized sales and marketing into a single team, and replaced half the top management. A major cultural change programme, run by consultants and centred on team-working, replaced the organization's former hierarchical set-up. Workshops were also arranged to facilitate the changes, but the training programme was interrupted by severe difficulties with the new products, deliveries, and customers. Sales dropped sharply, further demoralizing the staff, who were already dismayed by uncertainty and rapidly shifting priorities. Henry was removed, but too late to save the business.

EVALUATING COMPLEXITY

To plan and manage change effectively, you need to make a realistic estimate of its complexity and whom it will affect directly and indirectly. You then need to break down, quantify, and organize the various components clearly and efficiently.

28 Ask of every change, how will this affect all those involved?

29 Try proposed changes on a small scale first.

30 If it takes complex reasoning to justify change, abandon it.

BREAKING DOWN CHANGE

Analyzing the complexity of any programme requires a logical approach to reduce it to simple elements. List all the areas that will need to be tackled to complete a major change, and group related areas together into projects. Break these projects down into manageable tasks, ready for allocation to different teams. This should give you an idea of the complexity of the change. You may find it valuable to test your methods of analysis and organization on a smaller task before embarking on the main change programme itself.

ASSESSING BREADTH

To appreciate the complexity of a planned change, you need to know who will be affected by it. At one extreme, only one person or a small group will be affected. At the other extreme, the whole organization will be involved, and its investors, suppliers, and (very importantly) customers may need to be informed, too. Always bear all three groups in mind when planning a change. Look carefully at each change planned, and list everyone affected. Think whether or not outsiders are involved, and remember that a wide circle of employees and departments must be considered. The more people the change affects, the more complex the change programme will be.

POINTS TO REMEMBER

- Everything and everyone that needs to change should be noted.
- Individual responsibilities must be made crystal clear.
- Teams are the prime engines of almost every change.
- Communication with all interested groups is top priority.
- The case for change must be expressed in a short, sharp, well-supported document.
- The acronym KISS – Keep It Simple, Stupid – represents invaluable advice.

DOVETAILING TASKS

All tasks in a change project need to fit into a master plan in which their timings are co-ordinated. One way to assess a project is to plot the "critical path" for its completion: work out the order of interdependent tasks to set a framework around which other tasks can fit. Allocate tasks to different teams or individuals so that they can be worked on concurrently, saving time.

▼ **CRITICAL PATH ANALYSIS**

The critical path follows the longest chain of dependent processes – those that can be started only when previous stages are complete: in this case, tasks A1–A5. This path allows leeway in the timing of other tasks (B and C), which take less time to complete but which have to be finished by a certain point in the main path for the project to continue successfully. Missing a deadline can cause knock-on effects that disrupt the progress of the critical path tasks.

Task B1 (4 days)

Task B2 (5 days)

Leeway of 3 days

Task A1 (2 days)

Task A2 (10 days)

Task A3 (7 days): can begin when A2 and B2 completed

Task A4 (4 days)

Task A5 (6 days): can begin when A4 and C3 completed

Task C1 (4 days)

Task C2 (3 days)

Task C3 (11 days)

Leeway of 5 days

QUANTIFYING TASKS

Evaluating a planned change is much easier if you can measure it. Try to establish quantified measures of the current position and improvement sought. Use benchmarking (objective comparison with others, probably the best-performing outsiders) or targets, or both. Make goals as concrete as possible to allow you to assess the size of tasks accurately. Draw together these measurements of tasks and the results of your analyses of tasks and people to give a complete picture of the complexity of the planned change and its components.

31 Use critical path analysis to help plan tasks.

PLANNING WAYS TO INVOLVE PEOPLE

Those affected by change will vary in their attitudes and needs. Effective change programmes should be flexible enough to match this variety. Carefully plan whom to involve in setting change in motion, and in what ways to involve them.

32 Always get your people policies right when planning changes.

33 Use training as a deliberate tool to involve people in change.

CHOOSING A STRATEGY

Different situations require different strategies concerning how much and in what ways to involve people. Whenever possible, involve people fully in developing long-term objectives and planning for change, as well as in implementing plans. But if a situation is uncertain, avoid involving people too early, since this may cause unnecessary anxiety. In general, draw people in through education and communication, although in extreme cases you may need to resort to manipulation or coercion.

CONSIDERING RESPONSES

When selecting a strategy, bear in mind people's potential responses, and consider if you may need to overcome resistance to change. Study your list of people affected, in groups (shopfloor, middle management, and so on) as well as individually. Which key people need to be involved? How may people react? Who is likely to be enthusiastic about introducing change? What worries may lead others to resist it? Will people need new skills or training? Specify positives and negatives in detail, and plan and prepare any necessary action with as much care as the change programme itself.

QUESTIONS TO ASK YOURSELF

Q Have I involved everyone who should be involved?

Q Do I and my colleagues really believe that involvement is essential for successful change?

Q Has the case for change been communicated and understood?

Q Have people had the necessary training and preparation?

Q Have management layers been kept to a minumum?

DECIDING WHETHER TO INVOLVE PEOPLE

THE SITUATION

A manager is aware that working practices need revision, and can see an appropriate solution. She has to decide how best to plan and introduce the change.

THE SOLUTIONS

Whenever possible, the manager involves staff, setting up a group working party to develop solutions and plan changes.

If absolutely necessary, in order to maintain confidentiality, the manager plans changes alone, later informing staff of decisions.

CONSULTING PEOPLE

The greater the number of people consulted, the more information will be available for developing change plans. And people involved in identifying needs and planning change will be more prepared for a challenge, willing to work hard, and convinced of management's commitment to the workforce. Change that would cause unease if imposed by managers can be relatively painlessly introduced by ensuring participation in decision-making.

DO'S AND DON'TS

✔ Do invite suggestions from everybody.

✔ Do hold frequent formal and informal meetings.

✔ Do involve teams in planning as well as implementation.

✔ Do manage people's expectations with care.

✘ Don't make offers people cannot refuse.

✘ Don't keep unnecessary secrets or tell any lies.

✘ Don't forget that change should improve business results.

✘ Don't leave anybody out in the cold.

34 Apologize and explain if people feel ill-informed.

DELAYING COMMUNICATION

In highly sensitive situations (such as acquisitions and mergers), change cannot be communicated until it is a *fait accompli*. Changes forced from outside – new regulations, for instance – also do not allow involvement until after the event. In such cases, move to involve people as rapidly as possible once the news is out, and explain why you were unable to speak about it earlier.

UNITING THE GROUP

Planning for change is an opportunity to unite the whole organization, which may in turn trigger new ways of thinking and further change. For instance, a holistic Total Quality Management approach involves everybody, individually and in teams. Co-operation across functions as well as departments binds an organization together as a super-team, encouraging people to use a common change language and aim at common objectives.

35 Involve everybody in the planning of at least one change project.

36 Give all teams some autonomy in setting their own targets.

WORKING IN TEAMS

Introducing team culture where it has not been the custom can in itself be a powerful force for change. Set up teams to help plan and implement the changes, and establish team targets linked with the overall aims of the organization so that team members can see how their role fits into the wider scheme. Make change goals ambitious, specific, and measurable, and maximize potential by giving teams as much autonomy as possible at all times.

▲ **PROVIDING INPUT**
Your experience and knowledge can be invaluable to both senior management and junior staff. Be ready to give tactful advice and input as required.

MAKING A PERSONAL CONTRIBUTION

While it is important to empower and involve others, do not underestimate what you can contribute yourself. Set an example by being open to change, and be ready with advice if either superiors or staff ask for it. Never refuse to contribute, or respond to a question as if it is unimportant. Change is unsettling, but it is also an opportunity to grow: as people progress from producing ideas to actually implementing change, you are their coach, information provider, questioner, challenger, and facilitator.

USING KNOW-HOW

Internal change management often needs extra skills from outside your immediate department. If people elsewhere in your organization have experience of change, or expertise in a particular area, use their knowledge on either a permanent or a temporary basis. Look outside the company, too, even overseas. Many consultants specialize in change management and can play a major role in design and implementation – for a major fee. Shop around before picking a consultant: pay attention to references from former clients, and to the success of the change after the consultant left.

37 Commit any consultants to a clear brief and short timescale.

◀ **LEARNING FROM OTHERS**
Encourage people to work together across functions at every stage of the change process. Urge them to share knowledge of equipment, technology, and people skills.

38 If you make promises about change, keep them.

39 Imitate good sports coaches – encourage people to progress.

EMPOWERING PEOPLE

Help people to use their powers and extend themselves, rather than restricting them. Start by initiating immediate practical work, for instance entrusting a team with planning how to improve performance on a key measure. The team will need "enablers" – a steering committee for reporting, monitoring, and back-up. Led by this committee, the team will plan its own project and, after completion, identify further change needed, which will become the next project. Real experience of responsibility for projects is a much better means of empowerment than talk. People who achieve change through their own efforts will feel more powerful and be eager to generate more change.

CHOOSING A TIMESCALE

Different types of change demand very different timescales. As agents for change, managers have to aim for long-term goals and at the same time plan other, smaller changes that take only weeks or days to implement – especially in times of crisis.

40 Avoid being ruled by financial years: they are purely arbitrary.

41 Aim to introduce one new idea every week.

42 Encourage people to find new ideas for quick-fix changes.

MIXING QUICK AND SLOW

Change projects can last a long time – it is said that it takes 10 years to make dedication to customer service irreversible. But short-term fixes with quick results can be essential to gain momentum and sustain enthusiasm. A change strategy should include instant actions with quick, recognizable impact, mid-term changes introduced during the current year that may not pay off until the next, and projects to be planned and implemented over the long term. Within each year, combine quick fixes with projects that take several months. In times of crisis, you will have to introduce more quick fixes, and you may find that an organization can absorb more radical change than you thought.

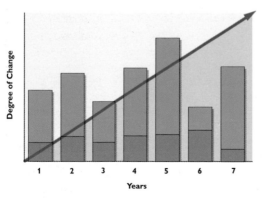

◀ CHANGE TIMESCALES
An organization's continuous lasting change is the aggregated effect of its specific changes each year. The amount of change varies from year to year, as does the proportion of quick fixes introduced.

Key

 Total changes per year

Quick fixes per year

Continuous lasting change

ALLOTTING TIMESPANS

Each type of change has its appropriate timespan. Complete any radical change as swiftly as you can to avoid prolonging upheaval. In a crisis, focus first on short-term solutions, then bring in changes over a longer period to deal with the causes. Continuous change, by definition, needs no set end-point; similarly, take a long-term view of organizational development and change aimed at growth. Change for competitive advantage may be fast or slow.

> **43** To make change easier to accept, plan to introduce it in stages.

THINGS TO DO

1. Think about future change programmes before the current one is completed.
2. Seek short-term fixes that sweep away grievances.
3. Set tight timetables and try to keep to them.
4. Build targets for continuous improvement into budgets.

STAGGERING CHANGE

There is a limit to people's acceptance of the new, and change is usually most palatable when it is broken down into stages. If your research and analysis suggest that people may find a planned change overwhelming if implemented wholesale, stagger the stages so that each does not begin until the previous one has been completed. This is often the most practical course of action. For instance, rather than introduce a change such as redesigning and renaming a chain of stores in a single initiative, "roll-out" the plan by proceeding in stages and refining the programme as lessons are learned.

MAKING QUICK CHANGES

To signal that change is on the way, try introducing some of the following:

- Abolish social distinctions between management and staff, such as reserved parking places or separate dining rooms;
- Set up a taskforce to review rules, forms, reports, and other bureaucratic items, singling out any that can be dropped;
- Shorten chains of command by making reporting structures more flexible and extending the limits within which people at all levels are allowed to take decisions;
- Replace outdated and incompatible office equipment with modern machines.

EARLY PERSONAL COMPUTER

MAKING AN ACTION PLAN

On the basis of the information you have gathered, create a detailed action plan. Keep it clear and concise, making use of visual methods of planning and scheduling. Take into account the opinions of people affected, and review your plan regularly.

44 Ensure that people's views are given full consideration.

PLANNING DETAILS

Detailed, step-by-step plans are essential for change projects. First plan an outline of the necessary stages, based on your research and analysis. Then fill in the details, using the list of tasks you compiled when evaluating the complexity of the change – updated if necessary. For each task, set down goals, identify a strategy for achieving them, and estimate how long it will take. Apply critical path analysis to decide the order in which tasks should be completed. Give responsibility for each task to specific people, and arrange any training they may require.

CHECKING CONTENT

Ensure that your overall plan and the plan for each stage answer the following questions:

● Why is change being introduced, and what results are expected?

● What means will be used to reach those results?

● What resources will have to be committed?

● How will the plan be communicated?

● How will behaviour have to change?

● Who will lead the programme and its parts?

● What stages will it follow, to what timetable?

● How will the programme and its progress be measured and monitored?

● What could go wrong; what happens if it does?

ENSURING VIABILITY

Involve people from other departments or disciplines as widely as possible in assessing your plan's viability. Adjust and update the plan in the light of the feedback you receive. Gather feedback on a regular basis, via meetings (large or small), focus groups, and surveys, as appropriate. This will help you and others monitor the suitability of your change plan, and allow you to make adjustments as you go along. Change plans must always be open to re-evaluation and amendment.

45 As circumstances change, adjust plans – radically if necessary.

BEING CONCISE

When creating a change plan to present to colleagues, make sure that your case for change and your action plan are concise and jargon-free. Avoid marring people's first impressions of the plan by poor presentation or misunderstandings. Describe the programme and its purpose succinctly, breaking down overall objectives into aims specific to units and to individuals. Say concisely what is expected at every stage, and explain how progress will be measured.

46 Make sure that your action plan is properly presented.

Manager explains, answering questions clearly and openly

Colleague takes notes of supplementary points or issues to follow up in future

◀ **EXPLAINING A PLAN**
The manager has prepared a concise document for colleagues to describe and justify the project and outline her action plan. She explains the plan clearly, to maximize understanding and useful feedback.

USING PLANNING TOOLS

Certain tools are invaluable when planning change as they show complex situations with visual clarity. For example, cause-and-effect diagrams, called "fishbones" because of their shape, show causes that have led to a situation that needs to change (the effect). Ask people in different sectors to suggest causes that may have contributed to this need, and analyze each to pinpoint the prime cause or causes.

47 Become proficient in any planning technique you decide to use.

FISHBONE ▶ DIAGRAM

This diagram shows a completed fishbone. To make one yourself, draw a "spine" and write the situation that needs to change – the effect – at the end. Add "bones" leading into the spine, and label each with a related sector. Write specific possible causes along the relevant bone, and invite people to add further ideas.

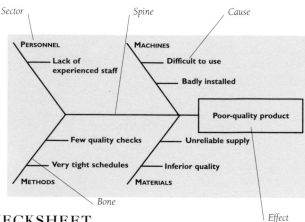

Sector   *Spine*   *Cause*

PERSONNEL
Lack of experienced staff

MACHINES
Difficult to use
Badly installed

Poor-quality product

Few quality checks
Very tight schedules
METHODS

Unreliable supply
Inferior quality
MATERIALS

Bone

Effect

USING A CHECKSHEET

It is important to be well organized and well informed when planning change: inadequate prior information is a major cause of failed change plans. Use checksheets to establish any omissions in your action plan. To create a checksheet, hold team analysis sessions, and make a full list of all relevant questions raised. Tick off each point on the checksheet when you are satisfied that you have devised a workable solution. If any points remain unticked, conduct further research to fill the gaps – they may prove to be vital. Consult your checksheet again after making your initial action plan, and revise it regularly.

48 Go over your checksheets at least once a week, updating them.

49 Always check schedules with those affected to ensure practicality.

USING A GANTT CHART ▼

This Gantt chart lists tasks on the left and people responsible for them on the right. The timescale of the project is shown across the top in weeks. Mark bars on the chart for each task from start to finish.

CONTINUING RESEARCH

The need to continue your research is often highlighted only after you have created your initial action plan. Omissions or weaknesses in the proposed change plan can become apparent when you look at the action plan in greater detail. To remedy any problems you discover, consult your original research material to find the source of the problem. Work from here, conducting fresh research where necessary, to devise solutions that fit in with the other elements of your action plan, and amend the overall plan accordingly.

Timescale shows length of project

Each task is listed separately

Member of staff responsible for each task is indicated

Bar indicates duration of task from start to finish

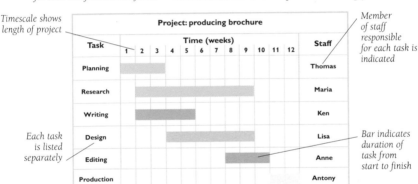

Project: producing brochure													
Task	Time (weeks)												Staff
	1	2	3	4	5	6	7	8	9	10	11	12	
Planning													Thomas
Research													Maria
Writing													Ken
Design													Lisa
Editing													Anne
Production													Antony

POINTS TO REMEMBER

● Cause-and-effect must be confirmed beyond doubt.

● Established work flows can almost always be improved.

● All factors relevant to a plan should be analyzed and charted.

● Change plans need to be built into line management's day-to-day responsibility.

● Effective plans cannot be based on inadequate research.

MAKING A SCHEDULE

When you have made your action plan, schedule it. A Gantt chart is a simple bar chart that gives a visual representation of a schedule, showing what happens when, who is responsible for what, and by what date. To fill in the chart, block in the requisite time for each task over the appropriate dates – it may help to refer back to your critical path analysis. Use the chart to plan and refine schedules, check progress, and anticipate periods that are likely to be particularly busy or allow little leeway for tasks to overrun or be delayed.

ANTICIPATING EFFECTS

Having developed an initial change plan, think through its consequences. Check that benefits outweigh disadvantages, assess all the necessary groundwork and requirements for implementing the plan, and prepare contingency plans as back-up.

50 Look for big improvements from change projects.

51 Include the prospect of individual and team rewards and recognition in a change plan.

ASSESSING REQUIREMENTS

The greater the change, the less likely it is to fit within existing parameters. For instance, an accounting system or software program that is suitable for one shop or office will probably be unable to cope with expansion to a chain of six locations. Use a checksheet to assess what you will need. Write down against each change activity the additional resources and skills it will require. Tick off each one when you have made preparations to meet that need – and if unexpected needs appear, move immediately to supply them.

LIAISING WITH OTHERS

The impact of a change programme can indirectly affect people outside your immediate department or organization. Make sure that you discuss your initial plan with these people, and liaise with them as much as possible to assess how the projected changes will affect them, and what you can do to provide for their needs. This may mean amending your basic change plan or adding further elements to accommodate secondary needs. By considering the needs of those even remotely involved with the change programme, you can minimize the chance of problems occurring later on. Removing barriers between departments in this way is, for most organizations, a massive change in itself.

QUESTIONS TO ASK YOURSELF

Q Have I ensured that everybody knows what benefits are expected from the change?

Q Does everybody fully understand and accept the case for change?

Q Can I answer everybody's vital question: "What's in it for me?"

Q Will the planned changes genuinely make people's jobs more interesting?

Q What would I want done for me if my job was at stake?

ENSURING IMPROVEMENT

If you are planning to reform specific processes, you should find that people are quite clear about what improvements on current performance to expect. However, if you are embarking on general restructuring, the consequences will often be less tangible. To double-check that the planned changes are likely to bring improvements, refer back to your original written case for change. This should list the issues, explain what would happen without the planned changes, and set out expected gains. Expand on these projections by listing the specific improvements that you anticipate from each reform. Wherever possible, quantify your aims, or link them to measures (such as customer satisfaction) that everyone recognizes as important. This will help to enlist and focus support for the reforms.

52 Never take people's support of action plans for granted.

53 Avoid the temptation to bribe people to change.

BENEFITING EVERYONE

Do not expect individuals to be altruistic. Each person will judge change according to what it promises or threatens for them personally. People rightly expect to benefit as individuals in return for the upheaval of making changes, so plan how to sell the benefits. If people can see nothing but disadvantages, you will not win their support. Make a list of everyone involved in planned changes, noting probable consequences for each person and how they are likely to perceive them. Then think about how best to present the changes and highlight the positive aspects. Emphasize any changes suggested by people themselves, as these are likely to gain support. You may plan to link some changes to higher pay or bonuses for better results, but people will feel most committed to a change project if you create a constructive working atmosphere by making it clear just how the organization's greater success will benefit everyone.

POINTS TO REMEMBER

● The likely consequences of change, inside and outside the organization, need to be considered thoroughly.

● All key managers must fully commit themselves to the change philosophy.

● Vital needs that must be supplied for a project to succeed should be identified and catered for.

● There needs to be regular liaison between all departments and functions affected by a projected change.

● Everyone should understand the importance of treating others as allies, not enemies.

● People at all levels are fully capable of understanding the business case for change.

54 Monitor morale closely, and act if it begins to deteriorate.

55 Avoid feeling sentimental over inevitable job losses.

MINIMIZING NEGATIVES

Any change programme will have negative effects as well as positive ones. Against your list of benefits, list perceived potential losses, and ensure that the benefits (to the organization and to the majority of individuals) are likely to outweigh them. When discussing the planned change, emphasize that gains (in areas such as customer satisfaction, more interesting jobs, and greater responsibility) will more than compensate for losses (for instance, heavier workloads). If people come to believe fully in the need for improvement at an early stage of planning, the chances are that they will welcome the change programme when it is implemented, and will be able to overcome their negative reactions to any disadvantages.

ANTICIPATING ADVERSITY

Dealing with negative aspects of change is a great test of a manager's motivating skills. In cases such as redundancies, people's living standards, security, sense of community, and self-esteem may suffer. Those kept on may also feel vulnerable about these issues. Prepare people by communicating as fully as possible, so that the need for change is understood, and by making plans for counselling and coaching for new jobs as required. Stress that change will improve people's chances of realizing their individual potential, either by developing a current job or by moving on to a better one. Make sure the plan will deliver on that promise for those who stay. Try to provide support for those who leave.

▼ OUTPLACEMENT COUNSELLING
If possible, plan for a counsellor to be available to give expert guidance and support to those facing redundancy. This should help them to move on in a positive way, both mentally and financially.

PREPARING CONTINGENCY PLANS

WHAT MAY GO WRONG	HOW TO PREPARE FOR IT
COMMUNICATION Team leaders are unable or unwilling to communicate properly with employees.	Ensure that coaching and seminars are available. If these fail, be prepared to replace the people concerned with new management.
FINANCE Projected cost savings from reforms are disappointingly small or non-existent.	Develop a back-up plan for further changes that will extend and deepen savings, and set up systems for tracing the causes of shortfalls.
IMPLEMENTATION People pay lip-service to change, but are hard to wean away from established practices.	Plan to remove old methods once the changes are introduced, so that there is no other option but to use the new methods.
COMMITMENT Feedback and observation suggest that enthusiasm for the changes is waning.	Set up systems for investigating the causes of the disillusionment, and be prepared to revise changes if necessary.
DELAYS The change programme begins to fall significantly behind schedule.	Establish checks to detect problems, as well as systems for remedying them and catching up with schedules or rescheduling as necessary.
THIRD PARTIES The programme begins to suffer from poor performance by a supplier critical to success.	Prepare for the possibility of setting up a team to study problems, and ensure that consultants are available, should they be required.
TRAINING The training provision proves seriously inadequate, in either quality or quantity.	Have outside help available to review training and set up new courses to remedy the situation as quickly as possible.
TIMESCALE Superiors, colleagues, and subordinates alike become impatient for results.	Be ready to bring forward projects that will yield immediate pay-offs, and make sure that their progress and success are publicized.
INTERDEPARTMENTAL SUPPORT You do not receive enough support from another department – for example, IT.	Arrange for people from other functions to be available for permanent secondment to work on the change programme as needed.
TROUBLESHOOTING Difficult, unforeseen problems arise and threaten to upset the whole plan.	Prepare everyone to treat difficulties as another challenge of change, and be ready to set up taskforces to tackle them.

ANTICIPATING RESISTANCE TO CHANGE

Change will always meet with some resistance. You can, however, pre-empt resistance to a large extent by anticipating and understanding people's reservations. Take steps to accommodate some objections in your plan, and gather evidence to counter others.

56 Watch out if no resistance is evident: it may be hidden.

ANTICIPATING REACTIONS

Try to see change from other people's points of view and anticipate their fears. Will they feel inadequately informed? Will they fear workload increases, loss of control, loss of status, or loss of jobs? People's reactions to an unlooked-for change tend to follow a recognized pattern. The initial response is usually negative: passive resistance is followed by active resistance and then further passive feelings, before eventual acceptance. Allow time for these reactions to take their course, and plan presentation and concessions accordingly.

POINTS TO REMEMBER

- Emotion cannot be countered by reason alone, but requires emotional reassurance.
- Once trust is lost, it is very difficult to win back.
- Criticism is not necessarily mere resistance: it may be well founded.
- Once a programme is up and running – and working – resistance will dwindle.
- In overcoming resistance, prevention is better than cure.

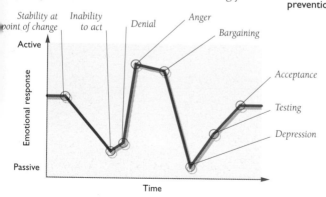

◀ **REACTING NEGATIVELY**
In response to change, people tend to go through a series of emotional reactions. Typically, passivity and denial give way to a fighting impulse, which in turn leads to depression, and finally to acceptance. The duration of this process depends on the particular situation.

BUILDING TRUST

Resistance to change takes three main forms: opposition based on misunderstanding or rational objections; fear of personal consequences; and emotional distrust. Prepare to encounter all these forms of alienation, and plan ways to deal with them. The intensity of negative response will largely depend on the existing degree of trust. So, before introducing a plan, be sure to consult and communicate with everyone as much as possible, to build up trust and prepare people for change.

> **57** Find allies who will help you to counter critics and conservatives.

DISCUSSING CONTENT

To back change, people need to understand its basis and feel involved in its development. You stand the best chance of forestalling potential resistance if your case for change is factual and watertight. Support your plan with facts and figures. Compare business processes accurately against competition. Be precise about market demands, customer perceptions, and competitive trends. Show why your organization cannot do significantly better without great change. Discuss plans in detail: incorporate any valuable ideas into the action plan, and ensure that people who make suggestions do not feel unimportant or ignored.

> **58** Always be frank about the possible adverse effects of change.

▼ SEEKING OPINIONS

When obtaining feedback, even negative opinions contribute to the planning process. Here, colleagues pay attention to each other's views, responding with interest and taking notes on major points.

Explains opinions openly and in detail

Takes notes of feedback and suggestions

Comments on colleagues' opinions

TESTING AND CHECKING PLANS

Without testing and double-checking, plans will be risky and will almost certainly lead to disappointing results. Use well-designed pilot schemes and experiments, together with methodical monitoring, to strengthen and improve your overall planning.

59 Test your plans with experiments in every possible context.

60 Allow for variable factors when reviewing pilot scheme results.

TESTING POSSIBILITIES

Pilot schemes – dry runs that test a plan, fully or in part – are ideal for trying out provisional plans without causing disruption to the organization or incurring major risks or expense. You cannot know, for instance, whether manufacturing cells can successfully replace assembly lines until a cell is actually operating, but you would not want to introduce cells plant-wide without being sure that they work. A pilot should produce significant pay-offs. It also serves to test and refine planning methods and implementation procedures, and may generate enthusiasm for change by giving people a taste of the consequences.

CASE STUDY
A company's service staff, when visiting customers, usually returned to get parts for major repairs.
The change team believed that altering this system could improve efficiency by 20 per cent and serve customers better.
They reviewed the whole system, finding that telephone diagnosis could handle a much larger number of cases than previously thought, thus cutting down on service visits. The change team also proposed halving head-office personnel, altering IT, and introducing measurement methods and incentives to support the changes.
The changes were piloted in three locations: return trips for parts largely vanished, and technicians doubled the number of daily calls. The 20 per cent efficiency target was met.

◀ **PILOTING CHANGE**
By using three pilot schemes to test new practices, the organization proved their viability and avoided costly mistakes. Proof of viability also helps to minimize scepticism and doubts about a plan.

DOUBLE-CHECKING PLANS

Regular monitoring will lead to modifications and sometimes radical departures from your initial plan. Do not take these as signs of weakness – a healthy change plan should always be adaptable and open to further development. Be sure to check, reassess, and update plans regularly, before and during implementation. In particular, watch out for unexpected knock-on effects and aspects that you may have overlooked earlier. Remember that contingency plans will also need updating, since the likelihood of some complications arising may diminish or unexpected ones may appear.

61 Analyze shortfalls in performance and find all the reasons for them.

62 Thank people for putting forward useful objections and criticisms.

Planned cut of 23 per cent

Actual cut of 5 per cent

◀ **REFINING PLANS**
In many cases, planned cuts are over-ambitious and unrealistic. If, in your enthusiasm, you overlook a key factor, you will probably find that the cut you achieve is much less than you planned.

QUESTIONS TO ASK YOURSELF

Q Have I used pilot schemes to raise enthusiasm for change?

Q Does everybody know what is going on at pilot sites?

Q Do I hold a weekly meeting (at least) to review plans?

Q Do I regularly revise contingency plans to eliminate the irrelevant and make new provisions?

Q Do I have a system for tackling major objections?

CHECKING OBJECTIONS

Use objections to help you double-check plans. When a change plan encounters major objections, analyze the reactions from groups and individuals. If you are told that part of the plan will not work, ask for evidence. If none is provided, conduct your own research to see whether the objection is valid, and on what grounds. Once you know the facts, consider whether rejection of this part of the plan would have serious effects, and whether there are alternative courses of action. Where you can find no means of overcoming the objection, develop alternative solutions if possible. Even shelved points can be useful: keep a file of overruled objections, and periodically check their validity.

IMPLEMENTING CHANGE

A change programme can be only as good as its execution. Communicate carefully, monitor progress, and prepare yourself for possible changes during the course of the programme.

COMMUNICATING CHANGE

To get a programme off to a good start, communication is vital: you can never communicate too much. Whether or not people were involved in planning, draw them in now as quickly and fully as possible, using a range of communication methods.

63 Remember that honesty is not the best policy: it is the only policy.

TELLING PEOPLE SOON

Make sure that all aspects of a change plan are communicated as soon as possible to everyone affected. Anything short of total communication will leave some people unhappily in the dark, at least for a time, and may create a divide between those who know and those who do not. Letting people learn of a major change plan from outsiders (for instance, suppliers or the media) is the worst possible introduction to the programme, since it creates an atmosphere of distrust and anxiety.

Colleague raises further points for discussion

GIVING THE FULL PICTURE

Always give people the total picture: if you tell them only what they need to know in order to fulfil their own particular role in a change plan, they may not see the wider significance of their tasks or feel commitment to the plan as a whole. If people know and understand the reasons for change, and how and why the change plan has been formed, they are likely to play their part with greater enthusiasm and sense of direction. To reinforce this awareness, you can distribute reminders – such as credit-card-sized memory aids – that summarize the objectives of a project.

64 Display concise vision statements to reinforce the change message.

DRAWING PEOPLE IN

The best way for everyone to become familiar with change is by action rather than discussion. To some extent, change projects generate their own involvement, since they require people to learn new skills and refurbish existing ones, thus drawing everyone in. But use workshops and meetings, in which managers and staff study the project and its implementation, to inform and involve people fully at every stage of the process.

65 Make training for all the centrepiece of any change programme.

Manager expands on points in written plan in response to questions

Colleague follows closely, adding notes to written plan

◀ **BRIEFING PEOPLE**

When communicating change plans to other people, combine written material with verbal explanations, filling in details as required. Hold regular meetings, and encourage others to offer ideas and get involved in the change project.

WAYS TO COMMUNICATE CHANGE

METHODS	WHEN TO USE EACH METHOD
MEDIA Pieces in magazines and newspapers, on your Website, and on video that signal change.	To create awareness and provide information so that people can keep up to date and think about the change programme.
PRESENTATIONS Presentations to large and small groups, supplemented by media as described above.	To sell a large-scale change programme and stimulate understanding, support, and involvement from all affected.
TRAINING Training sessions, ranging from management workshops to shopfloor-skills training.	To prepare those affected and back up a forthcoming change programme while simultaneously building committed support.
TEAM MEETINGS Full meetings at which people discuss issues, air problems, and suggest solutions.	To advance the change programme by involving everyone, allowing them to voice opinions and discuss progress.
TROUBLESHOOTING Regular feedback, team problem-solving, and progress-briefing sessions.	To maintain commitment, solve problems, advance and monitor the success and failure of the change programme.

66 Speak about change plans to as many people individually as you can.

CHOOSING METHODS

You face a wide range of options when revealing change decisions: choose your methods carefully. Use personal communication in preference to written notification, not least because people can ask questions. If some are likely to react badly, you may want to inform people one by one, rather than all together. Ideally, combine a number of methods, such as media, presentations, and team meetings, to enable staff to raise problems or suggestions. In large organizations, groups are often informed in sequence: top management briefs departmental managers, who brief unit managers, who brief unit members.

AVOIDING PITFALLS

Be careful not to create false impressions, whether positive or negative. Promoting excessively high expectations is sure to backfire later; arousing unjustified fears will have an immediate adverse impact. Be realistic, and do not gloss over any less positive facts. You cannot predict how people will react: seek feedback to make sure that the decision to change has been correctly interpreted.

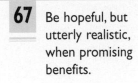

67 Be hopeful, but utterly realistic, when promising benefits.

BREAKING BAD NEWS

Communicating change often involves breaking bad news to people. This may be unexpected or anticipated, but in any case give people the facts as soon as possible – delaying an announcement merely prolongs the agony. Present the case for change with reasoned argument and supporting facts. Whether or not people expect bad news, they will understand rational and considered decisions. If they then disagree with your reasoning, on emotional or intellectual grounds, you need to look into the issues they raise. Consult your contingency plans to help you understand the basis of the problem, and take steps to address it directly.

68 Blame the message, not the messenger or the audience, for bad reactions.

DELIVERING NEWS OF ADVERSE CHANGE

Bad news is bad news, and there is no point in concealing the fact. Try to give positive explanations. Be sympathetic at all times (and apologetic, if need be), but make it clear that the change is unavoidable. Use expressions like the following:

66 *I'm very sorry that you couldn't be told earlier – this is the first opportunity I've had.* 99

66 *Nobody wants to make this change, but if we don't, our success will be compromised.* 99

66 *I would have liked to promote you, but the changed role requires a different set of skills.* 99

66 *Unfortunately the team's own analysis shows that your department needs major restructuring.* 99

ASSIGNING RESPONSIBILITY

By their natures, change programmes call for leadership. But they also require inspired, dedicated, and inspiring followers. Whether leaders or followers, "change agents", located in key positions, play an indispensable role in the change process.

69 Put change agents in place before launching a change programme.

DEFINING CHANGE AGENTS

70 Make sure that those leading change support it thoroughly.

A change agent is an enthusiast for change who can pass their enthusiasm on to others, and so takes on pivotal responsibilities in a change programme. Everyone is capable of great reactive change, but a minority are proactive by nature, relishing the challenge of change. In any change programme, but especially a prolonged one where continued enthusiasm is essential, identify potential change agents and place them in strategic positions.

USING CHANGE AGENTS

Change agents are valuable at any level in an organization, and also as outside influences such as consultants. Encourage change agents – especially subordinates in the thick of the action, who are extremely useful as examples and stimuli for others – and give free rein to their ideas. Change agents are often particularly valuable in meetings: they keep discussions going, take the initiative over suggestions and planning, and act as the conduits for delegation and for feedback from those undergoing change.

▼ QUALITIES OF A CHANGE AGENT

An ideal change agent is enthusiastic, restless, and eager for improvements. People with this kind of temperament stimulate eagerness for change in others.

Realistic

Eager for improvement

Effective communicator

Restless

Attentive listener

Good collaborator

Ideas person

DELEGATING CHANGE

Assign active roles in a change programme to various people at all levels, not merely to those you have selected as change agents. Break down every aspect of a programme for change, and entrust each part to a specified person. Designate these roles on the basis of desired outcomes – in other words, suit tasks to the skills and availability of a person rather than being constrained by their job description or rank. Ask yourself, "What final outcome do I expect from a person in this role, and who is capable of achieving it?" Make sure that everyone knows precisely what is expected of them at all times – having a clear role increases involvement. Also, check that everyone is confident about what they are expected to do.

Analyze the changes you want to achieve

Decide who should execute each one

Draw up specific tasks for each person

Discuss these plans with each person

Get feedback to check their commitment

---

71 Challenge any need for secrecy: avoid keeping information secret unless it is essential to do so.

SAFEGUARDING INFORMATION

People involved in a change programme may learn classified or sensitive information. In assigning roles, ensure that change agents understand about confidentiality, yet will keep secrecy to a minimum consistent with security. For example, if careless talk might lead to commercial damage (as with new product plans), security must be absolute. But within an organization, secrets are rarely that sensitive, and refusing to be open will damage morale.

DO'S AND DON'TS

✔ Do promote comradeship among change agents.

✔ Do give change agents stretching tasks that develop them for future responsibility.

✔ Do encourage people to form and follow up ideas for change.

✔ Do listen to what change agents say about morale and reactions.

✘ Don't assume that older people are too set in their ways to be change agents.

✘ Don't discourage others by singling out change agents for special treatment.

✘ Don't prevent change agents from using their initiative.

✘ Don't create an atmosphere of secrecy for its own sake.

DEVELOPING COMMITMENT

Building up people's support is essential for the success of change projects. Use strong leadership skills to gain and deepen commitment. Set the tone through your own dedicated attitude, and structure meetings and systems to stimulate and involve people.

72 Remind people that change is for everyone, not just a few.

73 Use your own commitment to change as an example for others.

LEADING THE WAY

For a change programme to succeed, all levels of management need to be involved along with everyone else. Do not let anyone think that change is just for others and not for them. Lead by example, showing your own commitment to the change philosophy and to this change programme: be ready to practise what you preach, and take an active part in discussion and implementation. Your whole-hearted personal involvement as a change leader, together with that of your colleagues, provides the best possible example and inspiration to subordinate staff. Make sure that your words and actions reinforce people's awareness of the benefits of the change and their commitment to it.

BEING FLEXIBILE ▼
A person who is flexible and open to new ideas is a good role model for others. To become more flexible, try to develop certain characteristics.

Is able to take a long-term view

Enjoys hearing new and different ideas

Relishes short-term success

Can ride through disappointments and setbacks

Looks forward to personal challenge

Is excited by trying new things

Can move quickly to take opportunities

74 Use regular progress meetings to highlight achievements.

▼ **GETTING FEEDBACK**
A team implementing change meets regularly to discuss progress. Make sure that the whole team is committed to change: take up useful ideas, and give and accept criticism in a positive manner.

TAKING UP SUGGESTIONS

Even if a change has been sprung on staff, you can still create a positive, committed atmosphere by involving everyone in implementation. That means being open to suggestions. A change project in which new orders are simply given and followed will not involve people or disarm their resistance. Be seen to listen to and act on people's ideas – this will increase motivation and improve performance. Set up small taskforces to tackle specific areas of the plan, and remember that small ideas can be as effective as big ones.

BUILDING DIALOGUE

In a well-run change programme, dialogue begins at the beginning, when change is first considered, and never stops. This maximizes commitment from everyone. Treat even resistance as a sign of involvement, and let it play a positive role in the programme: objections provide a springboard for no-holds-barred discussion, and often lead to improvements. As changes progress, encourage dialogue to continue informally, but also set up a regular forum, probably weekly, as an integral part of the process. Here progress can be reported and discussed, and problems and solutions identified.

POINTS TO REMEMBER

● Setting up a special suggestion scheme works well.

● Moving from following orders to a system of advice and consent is a major change in itself.

● Confronting opposition and opponents is a painful necessity.

● If obstructive ringleaders will not reform, they will have to leave.

● All senior people should develop the habit of talking and listening to everybody.

CHANGING CULTURE

The culture of an organization grows out of the behaviour of the people within it, and in turn it influences how they behave. Aim to guide the development of your organization's culture by various means so that it supports your changes.

75 Generate a feel-good factor by redecorating the place.

76 Err on the side of excess when celebrating a major success.

CHANGING ENVIRONMENTS

Environmental changes work practically and symbolically: change is often easier to accept if the physical and structural surroundings also alter. To encourage change within a department, for example, relocate it away from head office to new premises, reinforcing its sense of autonomy while encouraging initiative, independence, and interest in new ideas. Even a small change such as new decor can make a noticeable difference.

ACKNOWLEDGING SUCCESS

Any process of change takes effort, if only to forget old ways and adjust to new methods of working. Special effort deserves a special response. Spare no expense when celebrating the achievements of those who make outstanding contributions – this will encourage everyone. Use presentations, publications, parties, and personal praise and thanks to build an atmosphere of success and progress. But do not trivialize celebrations by holding them too frequently.

▲ **REWARDING ACHIEVEMENT**
When an individual wins an award, his success reflects well on the team. The recognition confirms his sense of achievement and encourages those around him to continue working for change.

WAYS TO INFLUENCE BEHAVIOUR

FACTORS	HOW TO USE THEM
GOAL-SETTING	Set personal objectives for people so that they focus their minds on performance; reaching the goals will reinforce their enhanced drive.
PRAISE	Commend people, publicly or privately, to strengthen commitment. Be sure to set high standards, and never ignore mistakes.
ENJOYMENT	Make work fun, with celebrations, outings, posters, awards, and customer visits to stimulate all-round involvement.
ROLES	Allocate temporary or permanent leadership or facilitation roles to encourage people to take a wider view and develop their skills.
REWARDING	Be willing to pay generously for achievement. People may change their behaviour radically for significant pay rewards.
CONDITIONS	Move offices, redesign or redecorate them, or use other physical moves to create a fresh atmosphere that affects behaviour.
PROCEDURES	Change the way you run meetings or award authority to reinforce new ways of relating to other team members.

LINKING PAY TO EFFORT

People want to feel that their reward will match their efforts; if it does, this will reinforce their commitment to the new ways. In some change projects, links between pay and performance are explicit: a team works to effect improvements, and proof of success lies in savings achieved, which are divided between the organization and the team. However, some experts say that such schemes miss the point of change, which is to move to better working systems. People still benefit financially by sharing, as teams and/or individuals, in the organization's growing prosperity.

77 Always attend if celebrations have been arranged.

78 Let teams decide how to share financial rewards.

LIMITING RESISTANCE

The greatest challenge for managers is to overcome barriers, especially emotional ones, to acceptance of change. While careful planning forestalls many problems, you will still need to interpret and deal effectively with various forms of resistance.

79 Make people feel their own roles are strategically important.

80 Treat people gently if morale is low during the change cycle.

DETECTING RESISTANCE

Resistance can take many forms, both active and passive. Watch for signs of resistance, and try to interpret them. Consult your change plan to find out what kinds of resistance you anticipated and how you proposed to deal with them. You should be able to tell from the type of resistance what stage a person has reached in their response to change, and whether their prime concerns are rational objections, personal fears, or general emotional distrust of change. This knowledge will help you to choose the best response.

ACTIVE RESISTANCE

If opposition is openly stated and clearly visible, it is active resistance. Opposition to the content of a project will surface in argument and criticism; this may be exaggerated, but deeper objections often lie beneath the surface. Investigate carefully through meetings or troubleshooting sessions. Personal and emotional resistance often combine to reinforce an aggressive attitude. You may notice this in active confrontation in discussions, unofficial opposition meetings, angry memos and e-mails, threats of industrial action, carrying out those threats, and even conspiracies to stop change in its tracks. Avoid hasty reactions to aggression: decide on the best response, and apply it calmly and firmly.

Passive resister leans back and folds arms, suggesting barrier against change

PASSIVE RESISTANCE

During a change programme, passive resistance can be just as effective as strident opposition. Successful change requires active collaboration: its absence may be a powerful restraint. Suspect passive resistance if you cannot find people when you want them, if they will not contribute in meetings or even attend them, if they hold back information, if they delay or block messages, or if they seem to block change while paying lip-service to it. Be aware that those who are not with you are against you, but do not interpret signs of passive resistance as final. In some cases, resisters will never be converted. In others, resistance merely indicates low points in a cycle of reactions that will eventually end in acceptance.

POINTS TO REMEMBER

- Objectors may have a genuine cause for their concern – resistance is not necessarily misguided or unreasonable.
- The ringleaders of active resistance should be identified and converted or made ineffective.
- Vague reassurances will not counter genuine personal fears.
- People will adjust better if they let off steam rather than having to hide their emotions.
- Resistance is best met with sympathy, without letting the situation become too emotional.

▼ FACING RESISTANCE
You can tell a lot about people's feelings from their body language. An active resister may raise his or her voice and use hand gestures, while a passive resister may lean back and fold his or her arms.

81 Take all resistance seriously, however far-fetched it seems, and deal with it effectively.

Manager leans forwards, showing interest in colleague's opinions

Active resister uses gestures to express objections forcefully

COUNTERING ARGUMENTS

Rather than bulldozing through objections that are based on rational arguments, refer to the facts you gathered when originally making the case for change. Turn the change plan into an offer that cannot be refused by stressing the positive potential of change and the negative risks if it is prevented. If anyone is still unconvinced, the first pay-offs as you implement the plan should raise enthusiasm and convince people of the wisdom of the new ways.

82 Set up a special suggestion box devoted to the change project.

ENCOURAGING DIRECTNESS

Always encourage people to express concerns openly, and confront those concerns as far as you can. If you ask people in groups, you may find that some leave the talking to others. Deal with this by going round everyone in turn if the group is small enough. With larger groups, call on selected individuals to speak their minds. In cases in which your hands are tied, explain why, express regret about it, and stress positive aspects of the change.

83 Be sure to investigate silence thoroughly – it is rarely golden.

USING MEETINGS

If ringleaders of the opposition emerge, confront them and seek to alter their stance. They may enjoy their roles and be most unwilling to relinquish them. Use one-to-one meetings to find a compromise. This must be to both sides' satisfaction, or the ringleader may provoke dissent later. Also hold one-to-one discussions with key people, and anyone who is especially troubled (even if less influential), and set up small groups to tackle specific areas of concern.

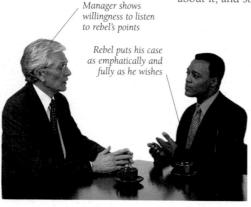

Manager shows willingness to listen to rebel's points

Rebel puts his case as emphatically and fully as he wishes

▲ **NEGOTIATING WITH A REBEL**
Hold private, one-to-one meetings with resistance leaders. Listen sympathetically, then combine direct persuasion, subtle coaxing, and compromise (if possible) to bring them round to the plan.

COMBATING FEARS

Be as straightforward as possible when you are addressing specific fears about the future of individuals. Speak openly about exactly what the change means for people, explain why you are certain that they can cope, and say why personal advantages are likely to outweigh disadvantages. General, vague emotional resistance is most difficult to overcome, since you do not share other people's emotions. Try to counteract negativity by being constantly upbeat and involving people in positive action that will produce quick-fix results – this will help to allay their fears and anxieties.

84 Persuade people that change will always mean opportunity.

DEALING WITH NEGATIVE REACTIONS TO CHANGE

TYPES OF NEGATIVITY	WHAT TO DO ABOUT THEM
RATIONAL Misunderstanding of details of plan, belief that change is unnecessary, disbelief in planned change's effectiveness, expectation of negative consequences.	● Explain plan with greater clarity and detail. ● Project what would happen if the change programme was not introduced. ● Involve everybody in quality-improvement teams to demonstrate effectiveness of managed change. ● Institute a bottom-up programme for reorganizing systems and processes.
PERSONAL Fear of job loss, anxiety about the future, resentment at implied criticism of performance, fear of interference from above.	● Stress much-improved job prospects for the future for everyone. ● Present plans for improvements which people are likely to find positive and exciting. ● Accept management responsibility for past failures. ● Present a scenario showing the anticipated benefits of the main changes.
EMOTIONAL Active and/or passive resistance to change in general, lack of involvement, apathy towards initiaves, shock, mistrust of motives behind change.	● Show, with examples, why the old ways no longer work. ● Stage a series of meetings to communicate details of the change agenda. ● Demonstrate that the new policy is not merely a "flavour of the month". ● Explain the reasons for change, and promise involvement. ● Be completely honest, and answer all questions.

CONSOLIDATING CHANGE

The implementation of change is just the beginning.
To ensure a successful change programme, develop processes
that constantly review and improve the changes.

MONITORING PROGRESS

*F*requent and accurate assessment of
progress is essential to ensure that a
change programme is effective. Simply
producing figures at regular intervals is not
enough: look at less tangible factors, too, and
compare both against planned achievements.

85 Only study or
produce measures
that clearly show
progress or results.

86 If performance
lags, look first at
how it is targeted
and measured.

MEASURING PERFORMANCE

What you measure is what you get. For example,
changing the targets for salespeople from measures
based solely on revenue to measures based on
profitability has an impact on the way they act to
achieve goals and on the actual profit made. Use
the financial and non-financial internal measures
included in your original change plan to focus
change and measure its progress over time.
Compare actual progress, in terms of product
quality and quantity, with planned progress. Make
use of external measures, too, such as customer
satisfaction, to chart the results of the programme.

MAINTAINING A BALANCE

Try to obtain a balanced picture of progress in all the areas that you set out to change. Schedules and measurements should give an indication of concrete achievements, but pay attention also to intangible factors, such as morale. Bear in mind, too, that one achievement may be worth little unless it leads to another – for example, increasing the rate of product development will not bring significant benefit unless it leads to an improvement in market share or profitability. But minimal progress in one sphere may be a worthwhile sacrifice if it means real progress in another, more significant one.

87 Find the few key measures that best judge success.

STUDYING ALL ANGLES OF CHANGE

EXTERNAL
Is customer satisfaction rising? Has the improved quality of the product increased sales?

INTERNAL
Is the organization or department meeting schedules and targets? How is employee morale?

PROCESS
Is quality nearing 100 per cent? Can schedules be cut? Are innovations emerging?

RESULT
Is market share up? Is cash flow positive? Are margins and returns as planned?

▼ KEEPING CUSTOMERS

A typical survey shows that around 90 per cent of customers who see your service as "excellent" remain loyal. Of those who rate it "good", 60 per cent stay with you, compared with 25 per cent of those who rate it "fair", and none who rate it "poor".

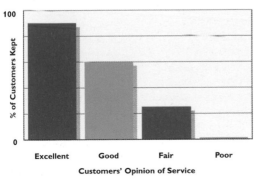

MEASURING RESPONSE

For most companies, sales performance, customer loyalty, and market share are basic hard indicators of the success of a change. But they do not tell why customers buy more or less, and stay or depart. For the answers, conduct surveys comparable to those used when originally planning change, to see what has altered. Even replies given in imprecise terms such as "excellent" or "satisfied" are useful, provided that the sample is statistically valid and that specific questions were asked. If customers rate you "excellent", the chances are that they will stay with you. But a huge gulf separates "excellent" from "good": avoid combining the two, or results will be very misleading.

REVIEWING ASSUMPTIONS

Change projects should not be set in stone: unless they are open to change themselves, they are unlikely to sustain long-term enthusiasm or to meet changing needs. Reassess long-term policies regularly – this is as crucial for success as initial planning.

88 Continually check a project's relevance to the changing environment.

REASSESSING OBJECTIVES

89 Do not abandon failing projects: reorient, revise, and reinforce them.

The objectives of change are not sacred: external developments can invalidate the reasons for a plan. For example, a radical rethink may be turned on its head by developments in technology. The more protracted a change programme, the greater the chance that the original plan's aims will no longer be viable. Revise aims every few months to ensure that sufficient progress is being made and that the aims remain relevant to external circumstances.

MAKING IMPROVEMENTS

There is every chance that revisions will strengthen the change process. Plans are based on assumptions and predictions, both of which may prove wrong. Once a plan has been tested by events, its weak points will show up and its successes will show what works and why. Even after the initial thrust of the change programme is over, continue to use feedback from everybody concerned to make improvements. These should bring economic benefits and help to sustain staff involvement.

REVISING A PROJECT ▼
Revision of a change programme requires data and feedback. Once a programme has been implemented, its results should be measured, and opinions and suggestions for amendments obtained from all involved. On the strength of this information, maintain or revise the programme, as necessary.

| Implement change programme | → | Measure results and obtain feedback | → | If successful, continue programme |
| | | | → | If necessary, revise programme |

REALIGNING PRIORITIES

Managers can be fickle towards change projects. They begin with great enthusiasm, only to cool off as time goes by and other projects catch their attention. When several projects are running at once, each has to fight for attention, and confusion – rather than co-operation – can result. Since projects may well overlap, the consequences are likely to be harmful. Make sure that your frequent progress reviews include an assessment of current attitudes towards and enthusiasm for each change initiative. Use these progress reviews to help realign policies that are no longer appropriate.

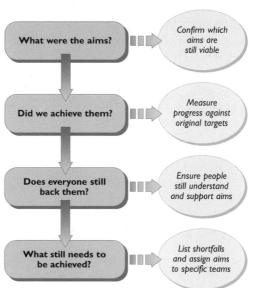

RECONSIDERING AIMS

What were the aims? → *Confirm which aims are still viable*

Did we achieve them? → *Measure progress against original targets*

Does everyone still back them? → *Ensure people still understand and support aims*

What still needs to be achieved? → *List shortfalls and assign aims to specific teams*

90 Avoid change overload: it can ruin the effect of individual projects.

91 Never assume that you know what people think – always ask them.

REVIEWING ATTITUDES

All change projects require changes in behaviour, which in turn flow from and create changes in attitude. Much effort may have been made to persuade people to support a programme, and as it unfolds, attitudes are affected by job experiences, personnel changes, successes, and setbacks. Even if people's behaviour complies with the changes, do not assume that all is well: attitudes can become negative, and this may eventually undermine morale. Use trusted people as listening posts, and stage no-holds-barred meetings or interviews. Then revise change programmes or re-stimulate involvement as necessary to ensure that people still support the change programme and its aims, especially aims that have been revised or replaced.

AVOIDING COMPLACENCY

Success carries a hidden risk. Having achieved excellent results through effective change, organizations easily relapse into complacency. This helps to explain why turnarounds, in which drastic change has moved companies from crisis to strong survival, often peter out. The same fate frequently strikes buy-outs, in which a management team, initially inspired into radical action, relaxes once the profits have poured in. The best change programmes always look two or three years ahead: to build on success and avoid falling into complacency, ask yourself what comes next. What are the new targets, and how are you going to meet them? What are you doing wrong, and how can you improve? Ask questions like these regularly to keep yourself alert and aware.

92 Keep setting stretching targets to move change forwards.

93 Ensure that revised objectives are communicated clearly to everyone.

▼ **TRACKING CHANGE**

This illustration shows possible positive and negative paths that a change project can follow. The project starts well, with group discussion and planning leading to implementation of new systems. Working practices improve, but without regular reassessment and revision the new systems become unworkable and fail. However, with regular reviews and amendments, the project's success is ensured.

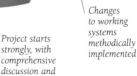

Changes to working systems methodically implemented

Project starts strongly, with comprehensive discussion and planning of change

BEING REALISTIC

In analyzing success, separate the impact of lasting changes in business systems from the effect of one-off events (such as large redundancies) or external developments. In a very hot summer, anyone can increase ice-cream sales: the important issue is whether your share of the booming market rises, and how your performance compares with the best competition. Similarly, the question is not how much money job cuts save, but the productivity of remaining staff. Even if you do well by realistic analysis, higher standards can always be achieved. Concentrate on improving weak areas, rather than just congratulating your team on their strengths.

94 Make the most of people who have played a key role in the success of change programmes.

Programme continues unchanged, and eventually degenerates

Programme is reviewed at regular intervals to meet current needs

CHANGING CONTINUALLY

The completion of a change programme should not be an end in itself. Because change projects normally have a definite beginning and end, the tendency is to regard the change as complete when a project is over. Special teams that have generated new product breakthroughs, for instance, are often wound up and their members dispersed. It is more beneficial to examine the procedures and processes that the group followed and to inject the best features and people from them into the rest of the organization. Promote change enthusiasts, and seek new projects that can utilize the lessons of success. Set these projects against a general background of continuous, company-wide improvement, and pave the way for change management to become "the way we do things around here".

MAINTAINING MOMENTUM

Change programmes are not unstoppable tides. They change course, stop, and start again. An organization's change momentum will eventually be lost unless there is periodic renewal, both for the specific plan and for those executing it.

95 Agree people's development objectives, and write them down.

REFOCUSING CHANGE

A change programme that does not itself change is a contradiction in terms. Think through the details of your change policy regularly, and refocus the programme if you see that progress is slowing. One way to refocus is to relaunch the programme annually, with fresh mission statements. Consider choosing a theme for each year, such as maximizing quality or improving speed, to focus attention on key issues and renew the thrust of change.

96 Use self-help guides to enhance your development and performance.

DEVELOPING YOURSELF

Whatever your status within an organization, you will always benefit from developing the range and depth of your own skills as much as those of your colleagues. Maintain the momentum of your personal development along with that of other people and the organization as a whole, and keep abreast of developments in fields that will help you to stay ahead of forthcoming change. Acquire new skills and broaden your horizons: read, listen to the radio, watch television, or use the Internet to tap further sources of information and ideas. Arrange to be sent on training courses that may not be directly related to your job (for example, outward-bound courses that build team skills), learn on the job (through trial and error), and take the widest possible interest in any business that is relevant to your organization. Constantly update your knowledge, seek out new ideas, develop your own initiatives, and be eager to plan and implement further change.

GOING OUTWARD BOUND ▶
Mastering unrelated skills, such as canoeing, can often have a genuine pay-off at work. It may, for instance, improve leadership skills, develop confidence, and build team spirit.

UPGRADING BUDGETS

If a change project does not pay for itself, something must be gravely wrong. Investing in improvements should increase profitability, thus justifying the investment and helping to make continuous change a fundamental part of corporate policy. Review budgets and resources regularly, and upgrade them as necessary to focus change where it can bring most benefit.

97 Set training targets for everybody, including yourself.

DEVELOPING PEOPLE

Change projects change people. Individuals used to following instructions develop self-motivation through directing their own work; managers who have never consulted staff improve their people skills by doing so. Build on these individuals' new skills by helping them look ahead, encouraging career moves, or widening roles. Let people take the initiative in such changes – this, too, will develop them.

98 Make sure that every change programme continues to increase profitability.

PROVIDING TRAINING

Education and training "from cradle to grave" is a key element in maintaining the momentum of change. Learning new ways of behaving and working enriches people's jobs and alters their attitudes. Some of the training will need to be technical, related to the specific tasks or techniques required in a job – for instance, mastering statistical methods or new computer software. But remember that people also need training in various interpersonal skills, such as leadership or team building. Whatever courses you offer people, impress on them the principle that everybody can learn improved or new skills at any point in their career. Make this way of thinking part of personal career plans, and see that these plans are followed.

BUILDING ON CHANGE

Change requires great effort. That effort is wasted if changes are abandoned or reversed, or do not form the basis for further advance. Successful managers plan for the future as well as the present, and make change part of their organization's culture.

99 Use strict and rigorous standards when appraising team performance.

100 Promote only people dedicated to change.

101 To be successful, plan, implement, revise, update, and build on change.

CONTINUING BENEFITS

A change programme at any level is often associated with a particular change leader, but should not be solely dependent upon them. Build positive change into all aspects of the systems and culture of an organization in practical and lasting ways – after careful research and planning – so that change programmes can continue once the original leader has moved on to a new project. In some cases, however, a new approach may be appropriate, so be open to fresh possibilities too, and do not allow success to make you inflexibly committed to the methods and values of the changes you have already implemented.

BUILDING ▶ ON SUCCESS
Tom, the team leader, identified the best way to maintain success in the marketplace – continuous change – and repeatedly emphasized it to his team. After he left, the team retained his methods and used their own initiative to continue achieving top-class results.

CASE STUDY
Tom had launched Project World Class with high ambitions. He constantly reminded his team that, unless they continuously adapted, they would lose their advantage and no longer lead the competition or delight customers.

Tom was deservedly promoted to another unit, but he was sure his successors would manage in the same spirit. In fact,

the team maintained the enthusiasm Tom had created – thanks to training, greater job variety, involvement in quality-improvement teams, and bonus payments. Many of the team launched and completed change projects using their own initiative.

Because everybody knew their targets and exactly how the team was doing, Tom's aim was achieved: "world-class" performance had become a way of life.

APPLYING SELF-CRITICISM

However good you are, you can always improve. Be sure to highlight your successes and enjoy them, but develop a habit of self-criticism, too – both as an organization and individually. As the best antidote to complacency, adopt a formal system of organizational self-appraisal. Draw up a list of headings, such as "customer satisfaction", "use of resources", and "innovation", and allocate 100 points between these headings according to their importance to you. Next, award your unit or organization a score (for example, 15 out of 20) under each heading, and add up the total: it will fall well short of 100. Then have a harsh critic – perhaps your manager – aggressively challenge your score. This process will reveal shortcomings and help renew efforts to improve continually.

▼ **CELEBRATING SUCCESS**

It is as important to enjoy the success of a change programme as to be aware of and work on its weak points. Do not hesitate to pass on praise and appreciation to staff, and share the fruits of their efforts.

POINTS TO REMEMBER

● New people should be expected to propose new ideas – that is part of their great value.

● Self-criticism needs to be allied with self-confidence to create a potent mixture.

● If people whole-heartedly support change, they will become its ardent defenders.

● Holding a "court-martial" from time to time serves to "try" your effectiveness.

● Any set-up should be re-examined and improved periodically.

INTEGRATING CHANGES

Always integrate a change programme so that each stage builds on its predecessors. For example, a marketing project that relies on next-day delivery has to be integrated with manufacturing change to ensure that orders can be completed on a daily basis. Continue to adapt organizational processes to help keep change alive – all set-ups eventually outlive their optimum efficiency. To prevent change from stagnating, change people's roles within a department. Move constantly forwards, and build each change project on to the last; in this way, the gains from change will continue to benefit individuals and the organization as a whole.

ASSESSING YOUR CHANGE-MANAGEMENT SKILLS

Evaluate how well you manage the demands of change by responding to the following statements, marking the options closest to your experience. Be as honest as you can: if your answer is "never", mark Option 1; if it is "always", mark Option 4; and so on. Add your scores together, and refer to the Analysis at the end to interpret your score. Use your answers to identify areas that most need improvement.

OPTIONS
1 Never
2 Occasionally
3 Frequently
4 Always

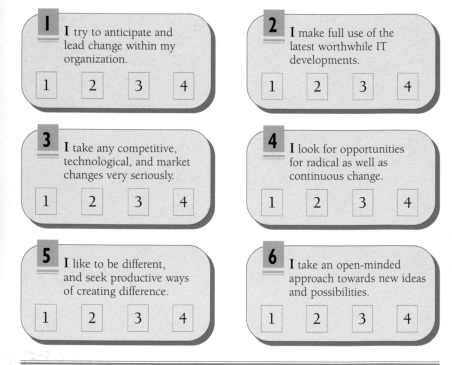

1 I try to anticipate and lead change within my organization.

1   2   3   4

2 I make full use of the latest worthwhile IT developments.

1   2   3   4

3 I take any competitive, technological, and market changes very seriously.

1   2   3   4

4 I look for opportunities for radical as well as continuous change.

1   2   3   4

5 I like to be different, and seek productive ways of creating difference.

1   2   3   4

6 I take an open-minded approach towards new ideas and possibilities.

1   2   3   4

7 I link change to any known needs of the customers.

1 2 3 4

8 I keep my change philosophy simple and concise.

1 2 3 4

9 I involve customers and suppliers in my plans for change.

1 2 3 4

10 I make a full and careful business case for changes and change projects.

1 2 3 4

11 I break change projects down into manageable components.

1 2 3 4

12 I consult widely in the process of deciding on strategy and action.

1 2 3 4

13 I obtain people's agreement to the actions demanded of them.

1 2 3 4

14 I use and develop teams as the basic units of change management.

1 2 3 4

15 I use quick-fix changes for instant results early in the change programme.

1 2 3 4

16 I plan well ahead for the long-term pay-offs of change.

1 2 3 4

17 I am careful not to create over-optimistic or over-pessimistic expectations.

1 2 3 4

18 I seize opportunities to reward, celebrate, and encourage successful change.

1 2 3 4

19 I make sure everybody knows the answer to "What's in it for me?".

1 2 3 4

20 I have effective and adaptable contingency plans available.

1 2 3 4

21 I anticipate adverse reactions and plan how to deal with them.

1 2 3 4

22 I use well-designed pilots and experiments to test my change plans.

1 2 3 4

23 I share relevant information with colleagues and staff as soon as possible.

1 2 3 4

24 I work closely with like-minded people who are keen to change.

1 2 3 4

25 My own behaviour is flexible and highly adaptable to changing needs.

1 2 3 4

26 I encourage people to speak their minds openly and to air their concerns.

1 2 3 4

27 I tackle resistance to change promptly, fairly, and vigorously.

1 2 3 4

28 I use quantitative measurement to obtain the results that I want.

1 2 3 4

29 I review and revise the assumptions that underlie the change plan.

1 2 3 4

30 I ensure that thorough training keeps people up to date with change.

1 2 3 4

31 I start the next change project as another draws to a close.

1 2 3 4

32 I use self-appraisal to check on myself and the organization.

1 2 3 4

ANALYSIS

Now you have completed the self-assessment, add up your total score and check your level of skill by reading the corresponding evaluation. However astute your change-management skills may be, it is important to remember that there is always room for improvement. Identify your weakest areas, and refer to the relevant sections in this book where you will find practical advice and tips to help you to establish and hone those skills.

32–64: You are resisting change or are unsure of its potential benefits. Overcome your fears, and learn to plan for change.
65–95: You understand the need for change – now you must develop your skills to achieve it successfully.
96–128: You are a skilled agent of change, but remember that change is a never-ending process, so keep planning ahead.

INDEX

ACKNOWLEDGMENTS

AUTHOR'S ACKNOWLEDGMENTS

This book owes its existence to the perceptive inspiration of Stephanie Jackson and Nigel Duffield at Dorling Kindersley; and I owe more than I can say to the expertise and enthusiasm of Jane Simmonds and all the editorial and design staff who worked on the project. I am also greatly indebted to the many colleagues, friends, and other management luminaries on whose wisdom and information I have drawn.

PUBLISHER'S ACKNOWLEDGMENTS

Dorling Kindersley would like to thank Emma Lawson and Jayne Jones for their valuable part in the planning and development of this series, everyone who generously lent props for the photoshoots, and the following for their help and participation:

Editorial Nicola Thompson; **Design** Kate Poole; **DTP assistance** Rachel Symons; **Consultants** Josephine Bryan, Jane Lyle; **Indexer** Hilary Bird; **Proofreader** Helen Partington; **Photography** Steve Gorton; **Photographer's assistant** Sarah Ashun; **Photographic co-ordinator** Laura Watson.

Models Philip Argent, Angela Cameron, Kuo Kang Chen, Roberto Costa, Felicity Crowe, Carole Evans, John Gillard, Sasha Heseltine, Richard Hill, Maggie Mant, Frankie Mayers, Mary-Jane Robinson, Lynne Staff, Wendy Yun; **Make-up** Elizabeth Burrage, Lynne Maningley.

Special thanks to the following for their help throughout the series:
Ron and Chris at Clark Davis & Co. Ltd for stationery and furniture supplies; Pam Bennett and the staff at Jones Bootmakers, Covent Garden, for the loan of footwear; Alan Pfaff and the staff at Moss Bros, Covent Garden, for the loan of the men's suits; David Bailey for his help and time; Graham Preston and the staff at Staverton for their time and space.

Suppliers Austin Reed, Church & Co., Compaq, David Clulow Opticians, Elonex, Escada, Filofax, Gateway 2000, Mucci Bags.

Picture researchers Victoria Peel, Sam Ruston; **Picture librarian** Sue Hadley.

PICTURE CREDITS

Key: *b* bottom, *c* centre, *l* left, *r* right, *t* top
Ace Photo Library: Andrew Conway 59*bl*; **Hulton Getty Picture Collection** 7*bl*;
The Image Bank: David de Lossy 65*cr*; **The Stock Market** 7*br*;
Telegraph Colour Library: Terry McCormick 50*br*;
Tony Stone Images: Frank Herholdt 4, Tony Latham 36*br*, Michael Rosenfeld 27*cr*.
Front cover **The Image Bank** *tl*.

AUTHOR'S BIOGRAPHY

Robert Heller is a leading authority in the world of management consultancy and was the founding editor of Britain's top management magazine, *Management Today*. He is much in demand as a conference speaker in Europe, North and South America, and the Far East. As editorial director of Haymarket Publishing Group, Robert Heller supervised the launch of several highly successful magazines such as *Campaign*, *Computing*, and *Accountancy Age*. His many acclaimed – and worldwide best-selling – books include *The Naked Manager*, *Culture Shock*, *The Age of the Common Millionaire*, *The Way to Win* (with Will Carling), *The Complete Guide to Modern Management*, and *In Search of European Excellence*.